SALT

Goldfish Press
4545 42nd Avenue SW
Suite 211
Seattle, WA 98116-4243

Manufactured in the United States of America

ISBN 13: 978-1-950276-06-6
ISBN 10: 1-950276-06-6

Photo credit: David Fontana

Book and cover design by Koon Woon

SALT

Poems based on a dream that mollusks and
bi-valves can suddenly sing

Goldfish Press
Seattle

For my beloved family,
for David and Josh, Margaret and Petra

Contents:

"…The lighted star-foam flows

There is no absence that cannot be replaced."

--René Char, "Chain"

The Barnacle

In a six-walled shell, white
and calcareous as a hollow tooth,
I am cemented

to the rock on my back.
At the tide change,
the operculum doors

slide open, I send my six pairs
of dark feathers to beat
like flames against the waters

to draw the ocean in
where I wait,
like a black robed monk in his cell.

The Geoduck's Song

Laugh if you will,
I am lovely to some.
A giant among clams

have I said I love sand,
a little thick mud?
A blanket of seaweed

keeps sea gulls away.
I live for the tide,
it brings me my life.

O sweet salt, I sing
through my long rubber hose,
a neck, not a nose.

A perfect periscope,
although I am blind.
I feel the vibrato of rain.

One day I will sing
Basso Profundo
in a chorus

of mollusks and bivalves.
We shall sing the great
Te Deum in the key of C.

A Dream

The night brain sings in it's shell
like a fat clam, all ooze and clamor.
Mollusks and fins crank and turn.

I hear their songs under the wave wash,
splash and gurgle. They wake
to sing the music of eons, an opera of brine.

The chorus goes on until first light
in soft sounds of windwave,
fades at dawn on an in-coming tide.

The Oyster's Song

I sing of the sea, its wash and tickle,
of sea wrack and sea worms,
surf smelt and sea weed.
I sing flute songs in all scales.

Once I sang tenor, virile and slim.
Now full-fleshed and female
I fill octaves with song.
My shell is baroque.

I lie on a chaise.
Delicate ruffles fringe
my pale body, filtering,
feeding me. I grow fat.

So sing with me, sisters
of the echo of shell light
dear little brothers,
all oysters together

sing hosannas with me.

Mussels

We are the colonists nestled among the barnacles,
indigo-purple robed choristers,
tethered by our green beards
to the rocks, where we multiply,
chant sutras at the turn of the tide.

When we open, the pale colors
of sunrise glow iridescent.
Sometimes in moonlight
we hum the blues soft and low.
At the Awakening our voices
will fill the air, rise like incense to heaven,
our shells clicking wildly like castanets.

The Mud Worm's Music

From deep in the muck

    layers of harmonics

        as if the mud were singing.

Mud worms hum

    as they wriggle and turn.

The ground quivers, pulses,

    and even those without ears

        (like the worms)

        listen

and the long dead perk up a bit

    to hear the worm's song

with jazz variations.

Moon Snail's Song

I am round as a baker's bun,
pale as the *Luna*.
I shaped myself as on a wheel

whorl after whorl.
I am plowman and predator,
feared for my appetite.

I burrow deep into sand
for the butter clam
horse clam and razor.

Each bivalve
I envelop, smother,
drag to the surface

suck out the creature.
See all around
the drilled shells of my prey?

A most murderous
mollusk, I sing Basso
and dark harmony.

The Horse Clam's Aria

I'm known for my largesse---
called "Gaper"
for my girth's exposed.

My shell is a tight fit.
I share my skirt mantle
with two pea crab who clean it.

I'm content in this muck,
let the world come to me.
Each wave brings newness in the brine.

I have tasted the oceans of India and Japan,
and once something very nice
from the sea of Madagascar.

Summer Time Age Ten, A Waking Dream

Wasn't there a small café – the scent of coffee?
a sweet smelling lilac tree on an empty lot,
blooms I purloined, or not?

It was all there- a house
where we once lived looking out to the bay,
neighbors whose ways we learned by heart,

a familiar row of look-a-like cottages,
like the faces of aging aunts.
Warm veils of summer. Fern draped trails to the beach.

And ramshackle Seaview Avenue,
sagging shacks with stuttering shutters.
Salt air coming up from the sea.

And wasn't the beach alive with the miracle of sand---
its myriad universes?
We were all plot and meander

among rocks and quarries. Sky the color of fish fins.
Everything crawled and bubbled in tide pools,
crabs and crustaceans, tiny finny fish.

Such were our dominions among the smallest things.
And didn't our pride grow in the toughness of our feet
as they hardened over shoeless summers?

I remember the long bus ride
into town and at the last minute, with the bus coming,
Mother dabbing at my face

with her handkerchief, moistened
for a moment in her mouth- that ancient ritual-
O the coolness, the scent of Yardley's lavender and lilac.

Aurelia

Moon jellies swarm in August
when the sea is warm.
Bloomy by nature,
they flourish in sunshine.

Overnight they are here.
A smack of them come
with summer plankton,
translucent, gelatinous.

Like alien space ships
they arrive overnight.
Transparent,
they bring no news.

They drift and go
nowhere together.
Then they are gone,
leaving only an absence.

The Giant Plumose Anemones

In a garden of sea flowers
we bloom white
on muscled stalks.

Our tentacles sting and gather,
as we sing a cappella
in the half light of water.

We hum in pale voices.
Like hunters, we wear feathered crowns,
for we must kill to eat.

Sand Dollar

The sand dollar glides on multitudes
of purple velvet feet among
the bleached discs of its dead.

They shine like pirate booty in the sun.
Missionaries claim they see written
on them the miracle of the cross.

I have never heard one hymning,
but they can clone themselves
when threatened by a pout-pout fish.

The Whelk's Song

I'm a rarity
among the round,
a spiral
wound tight
in a cobbled cocoon.
A vertical shell,
slender and small
I move on my slime
or stay clustered in beds
with other sea snails.
I fear the sea star
who hunts me,
to suck
my shell
dry.

Star Fish

The stars of the Pacific
Asterias rubens glow red
among the sea grass. They aim

knobbed spines at the heavens:
Alpha Centuri, Procyon
as if to signal their astral sisters.

As if blind stars could see
a faint glow of phosphorus
blinking up from the sand.

The message is urgent.
We are dying here.
Dying.

The Scallop's Song

Once I was the darling
of the Renaissance,
admired not for my thirty two blue eyes,
but for my fan shape,
like the setting sun.

I am a soprano---
perform all the old arias.
While my cousin bivalves,
the sedentary sessiles,
never go anywhere,

I wander at will
amid the seagrass
along the sea bottom.
I dance the *Habanera*
clapping and singing.

Kelp

Never good children,
it was the bulb we prized.
The *holdfast*, a tough handle

for the sea weed whip.
Its cruel lick against a bare leg
made tyrants of us.

In our hands such power
as we had never known.
Under rocks, the crab's

small kingdoms we conquered,
took captives home in a jar.
Shrimp colonies fell to us.

We viewed without pity
dead carcasses of gulls,
half-eaten bodies of salmon

with empty eye holes.
In the harsh sun,
the fresh aroma of salt, of rot.

How It Begins

In the sea's warm soup
a single cell lit up, a protozoa
floated a tiny candle,
divided into countless numbers.

Eons passed. Anemones came,
sponges and jelly fish,
echinoderms and ectoderms
with salt in their circuits.

Some crawled, some burrowed.
Some grew on rocks
from newly formed volcanoes.
An ocean jungle sprouted

a forest of kelp and sea grass.
Now beings with skeletons and fins.
Silvery fish learned to swim,
darted among them.

And an amphibian chanced
to walk on the cooling earth
between the water and the sky,
with the taste of salt in her mouth,
salt in her blood.

The Sea Shell

I hold it to my ear,
hear what it says about longing,
the terrible grief of being human,
listen to the tumble and pull
of wave and wind.

The earth eats us up bit by bit.
I must pack my bags,
find my way to the sea.
Gulls call to me like sisters,
the heron fishes on her high stilts.

Tide washes the beach every day.
Fish drink and drink,
but the ocean gets no smaller.
Let me be old here.
I will eat clouds.

Acknowledgements

"Mussels" appeared in *Pontoon*, Volume 11 2016

"Barnacle" and "Geoduck" will appear in the *Chrysanthemum 2020 Poetry Anthology*

About the Author

Sigrun Susan Lane's previous chapbook is *Little Bones* published by Goldfish Press. Lane's poems have appeared in *Arnazella, Albatross, Blue Collar Review, Bellowing Ark, Cascade, Chrysanthemum, Crab Creek Review, Cirque, Hubbub, Floating Bridge Press, The Mom Egg, Malahat Review, Melusene, Passager, The Poeming Pigeon, Pontoon, Rain City Review, Raven Chronicles, Sing Heavenly Muse, Seattle Review, Still Crazy, Stringtown* and other journals.

She has received awards for her poetry from the Seattle and the King County Arts Commissions. A widely traveled poet of Icelandic heritage, she lives in Seattle, Washington. She is a docent for the Frye Art Museum.